Abba

Wise Publications
London/ New York/ Paris/ Sydney/
Copenhagen/ Madrid

Exclusive Distributors:
Music Sales Limited
14/15 Berners Street, London W1T 3LJ, England.
Music Sales Pty Limited
20 Resolution Drive, Caringbah, NSW 2229, Australia.

This book © Copyright 1993 by
Wise Publications
Order No. AM91038
ISBN 0-7119-3362-6

Music processed by Interactive Sciences Limited, Gloucester
Cover designed by Hutton Staniford
Music arranged by Stephen Duro
Compiled by Peter Evans

Photographs courtesy of:
London Features International

Your Guarantee of Quality:
As publishers, we strive to produce every book to the highest commercial standards.

All the music has been freshly engraved and the book has been carefully designed to minimise awkward page turns and to make playing from it a real pleasure.

Particular care has been given to specifying acid-free, neutral-sized paper which has not been elemental chlorine bleached but produced with special regard for the environment. Throughout, the printing and binding have been planned to ensure a sturdy, attractive publication which should give years of enjoyment.

If your copy fails to meet our high standards, please inform us and we will gladly replace it.

Dancing Queen

Words & Music by Benny Andersson, Stig Anderson & Bjorn Ulvaeus

Strong rock

6

Does Your Mother Know

Words & Music by Benny Andersson & Bjorn Ulvaeus

Fernando

Words & Music by Benny Andersson, Stig Anderson & Bjorn Ulvaeus

Moderately

Gimme! Gimme! Gimme!
(A Man After Midnight)

Words & Music by Benny Andersson & Bjorn Ulvaeus

I Have A Dream

Words & Music by Benny Andersson & Bjorn Ulvaeus

Moderately

Lay All Your Love On Me

Words & Music by Benny Andersson & Bjorn Ulvaeus

Mamma Mia

Words & Music by Benny Andersson, Stig Anderson & Bjorn Ulvaeus

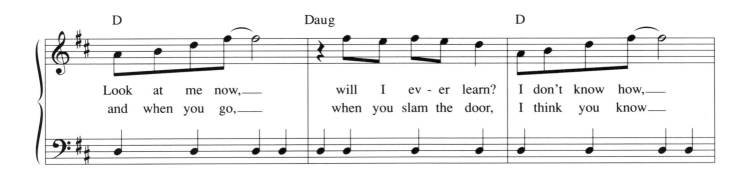

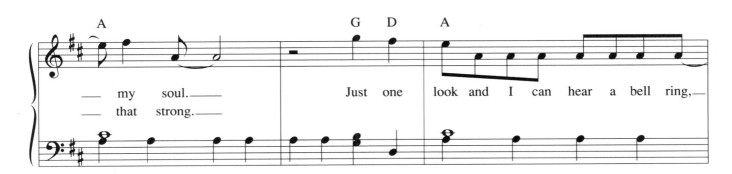

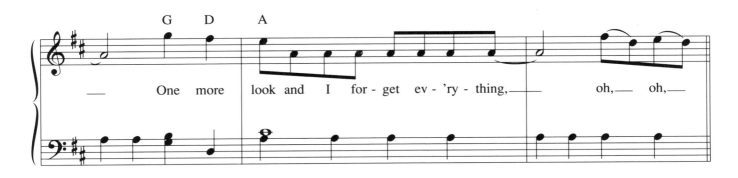

Money, Money, Money

Words & Music by Benny Andersson & Bjorn Ulvaeus

Steady 4

27

S.O.S.

Words & Music by Benny Andersson, Bjorn Ulvaeus & Stig Anderson

Super Trouper

Words & Music by Benny Andersson & Bjorn Ulvaeus

I was sick and tired of ev-ery-
Fac-ing twen-ty thou-sand of your

thing when I called you last night from Glas-gow.
friends, how can an-y-one be so lone-ly.

All I do is eat and sleep and sing, wish-ing ev-ery show was the
Part of a suc-cess that nev-er ends, still I'm think-ing a-bout you

last show.
on-ly.
So i-ma-gine I was glad to hear you're com-ing,
There are mo-ments when I think I'm go-ing cra-zy,

sud-den-ly I feel al-right, and it's gon-na be so
but it's gon-na be al-right, ev-'ry-thing will be so

like I al-ways do, 'cause some-where in the crowd ___ there's some-where in the crowd ___ there's you. So I'll be there when you ar-rive, the sight of you will prove to me I'm still a-live and when you take me in your arms and hold me tight I know it's gon-na mean so much to-night. ___

Take A Chance On Me

Words & Music by Benny Andersson & Bjorn Ulvaeus

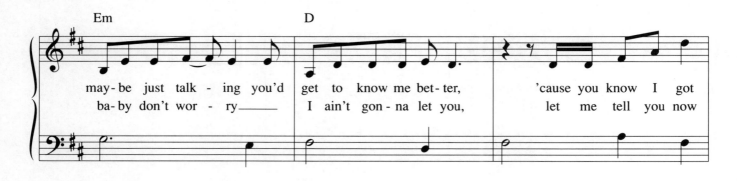

Em   D

may-be just talk - ing you'd get to know me bet-ter, 'cause you know I got

ba-by don't wor - ry____ I ain't gon-na let you, let me tell you now

Bm   G   Bm G

so much that I wan-na do, when I dream I'm a-lone with you, it's ma-gic.___

my love is___ strong e-nough to___ last when___ things are rough, it's ma-gic.___

Bm   G

You want me to leave it there, a-fraid of a___ love af-fair, but I

You say that I waste my time, but I can't get you off my mind, no I

Em   A   Em7   A

think you know___ that I can't let go.___ If you change your mind___

can't let go___ 'cause I love you so.___

D

___ I'm the first in line,___ hon-ey I'm still free,___ take a chance on me,___

36

Thank You For The Music

Words & Music by Benny Andersson & Bjorn Ulvaeus

Voulez Vous

Words & Music by Benny Andersson & Bjorn Ulvaeus

Knowing Me, Knowing You

Words & Music by Benny Andersson, Stig Anderson & Bjorn Ulvaeus

Waterloo

Words & Music by Benny Andersson, Stig Anderson & Bjorn Ulvaeus

Printed by Printwise (Haverhill) Limited, Suffolk 7/09 (170225)